CHRISTMAS REFLECTIONS

15 CALMING CAROLS ARRANGED FOR EASY PIANO SOLO

by Phillip Keveren

— PIANO LEVEL —
EARLY INTERMEDIATE

ISBN 978-1-70514-111-3

Visit Hal Leonard Online at
www.halleonard.com

Visit Phillip at
www.phillipkeveren.com

Contact us:
Hal Leonard
7777 West Bluemound Road
Milwaukee, WI 53213
Email: info@halleonard.com

In Europe, contact:
Hal Leonard Europe Limited
42 Wigmore Street
Marylebone, London, W1U 2RN
Email: info@halleonardeurope.com

In Australia, contact:
Hal Leonard Australia Pty. Ltd.
4 Lentara Court
Cheltenham, Victoria, 3192 Australia
Email: info@halleonard.com.au

PREFACE

This collection was originally published in 1997 as *New Age Christmas*. Since the book went out of print some years ago, I have received e-mails every Yuletide season asking "where has this book gone?!" Well, at long last, here it is – spruced up with fresh engravings and a new title, *Christmas Reflections*. So, reflect I will do.

In 1997, Lisa and I were parents to a 9-year-old and a 7-year-old. In 2021, they are both married, and we have two beautiful grandchildren. Tennessee has replaced California as our home. So many loved ones are no longer with us. But, come December, Christmas will come 'round again, and the carols we know and love will be ringing everywhere. We'll be looking at the season through the sparkling eyes of the youngsters in our family. Counting blessings, grateful for God's faithfulness in seeing us through good times and bad.

May these songs of the season bring you joy as you bring them to life at the piano!

Merry Christmas,

Phillip Keveren

BIOGRAPHY

Phillip Keveren, a multi-talented keyboard artist and composer, has composed original works in a variety of genres from piano solo to symphonic orchestra. He gives frequent concerts and workshops for teachers and their students in the United States, Canada, Europe, and Asia. Mr. Keveren holds a B.M. in composition from California State University Northridge and a M.M. in composition from the University of Southern California.

CONTENTS

ANGELS WE HAVE HEARD ON HIGH

19th Century French Carol
Arranged by Phillip Keveren

Flowing

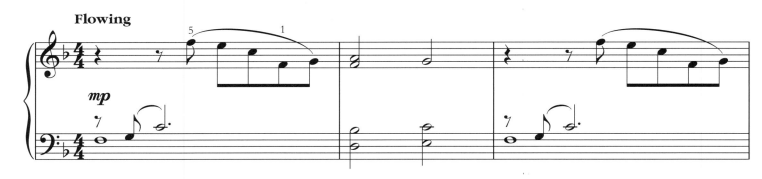

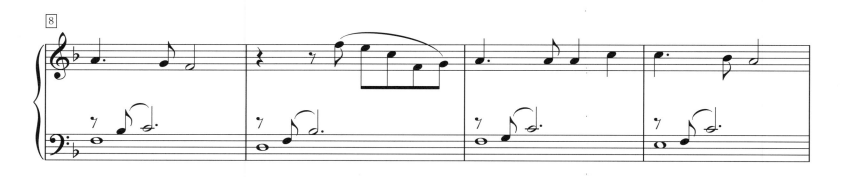

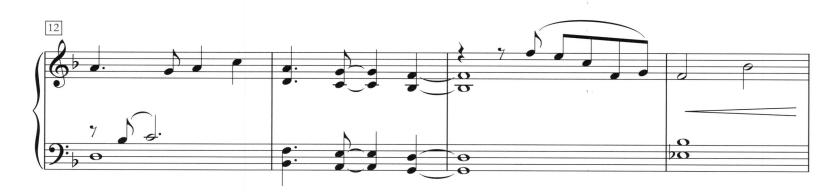

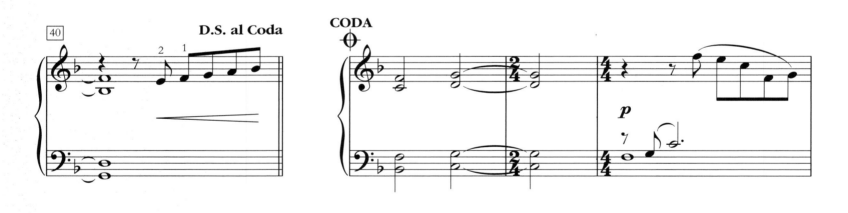

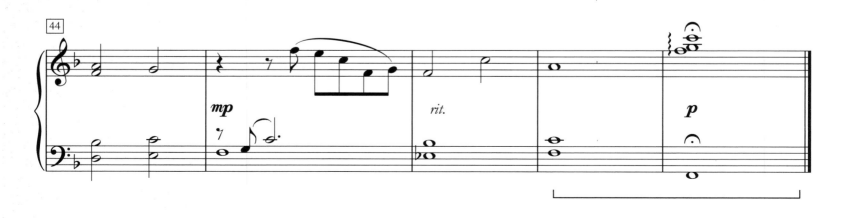

THE FIRST NOEL

17th Century English Carol
Music from W. Sandys' *Christmas Carols*
Arranged by Phillip Keveren

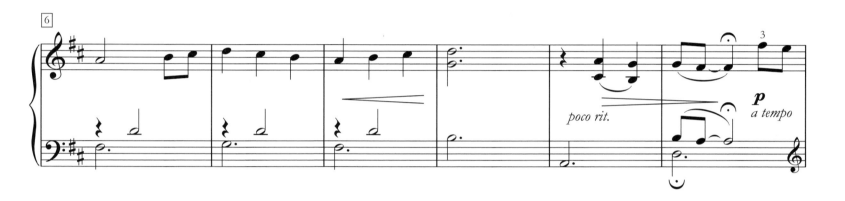

AWAY IN A MANGER

Traditional
Music by WILLIAM J. KIRKPATRICK
Arranged by Phillip Keveren

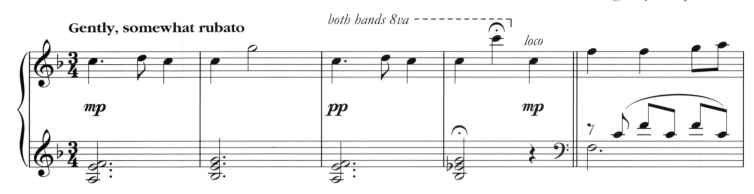

11

BRING A TORCH, JEANNETTE, ISABELLA

17th Century French Provençal Carol
Arranged by Phillip Keveren

With brisk energy (in "one")

mf

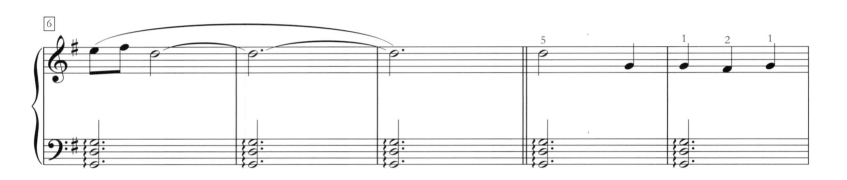

f detached

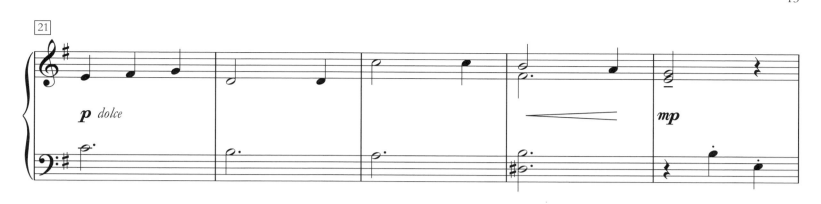

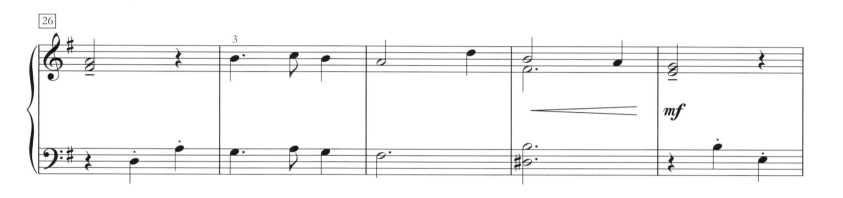

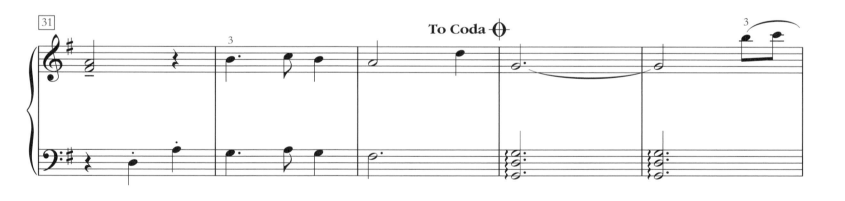

14

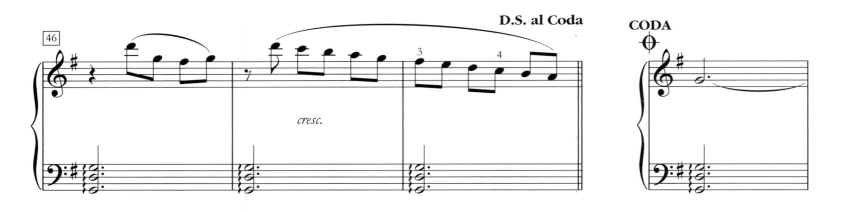

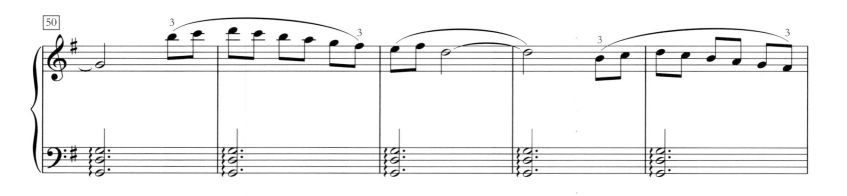

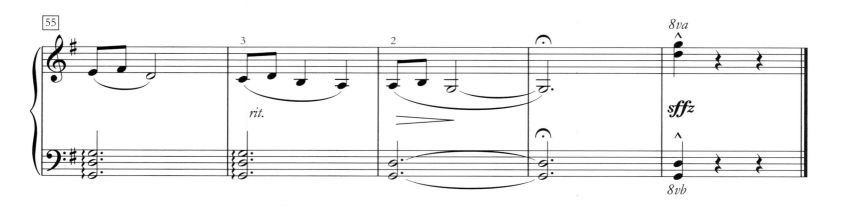

JOY TO THE WORLD

Words by ISAAC WATTS
Music by GEORGE FRIDERIC HANDEL
Arranged by Phillip Keveren

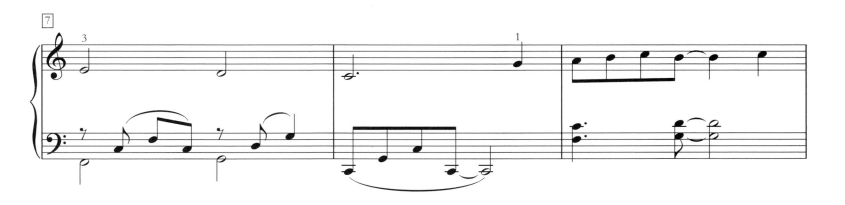

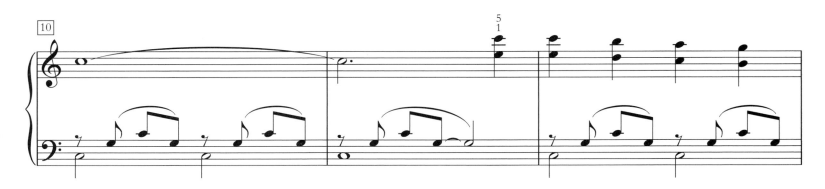

DECK THE HALL

Traditional Welsh Carol
Arranged by Phillip Keveren

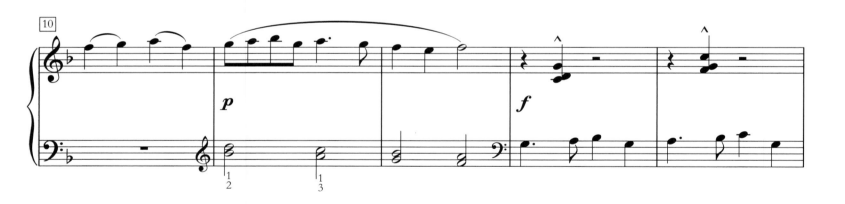

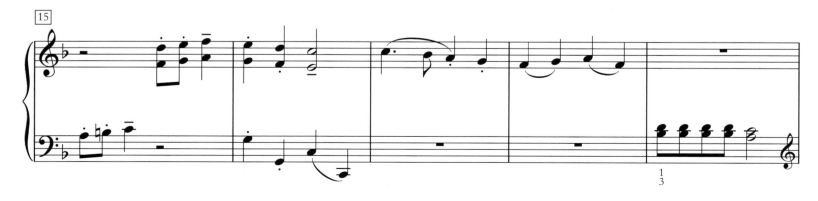

THE HOLLY AND THE IVY

18th Century English Carol
Arranged by Phillip Keveren

Unhurried

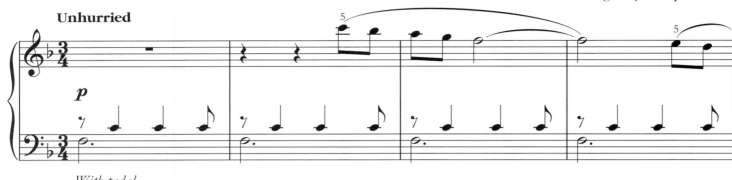

With pedal

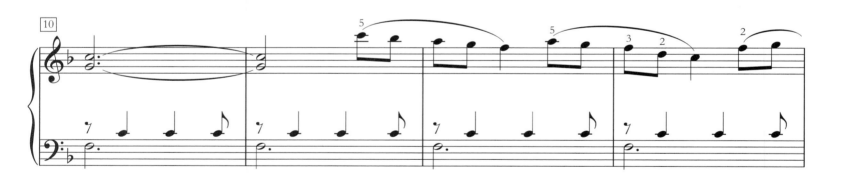

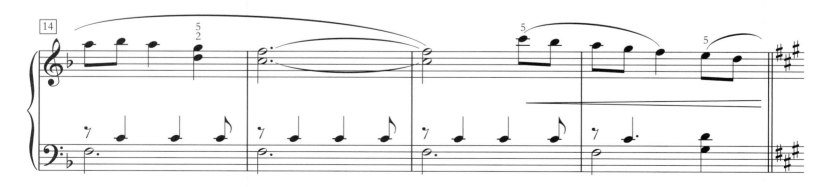

21

INFANT HOLY, INFANT LOWLY

Traditional Polish Carol
Arranged by Phillip Keveren

IT CAME UPON
THE MIDNIGHT CLEAR

Words by EDMUND H. SEARS
Music by RICHARD STORRS WILLIS
Arranged by Phillip Keveren

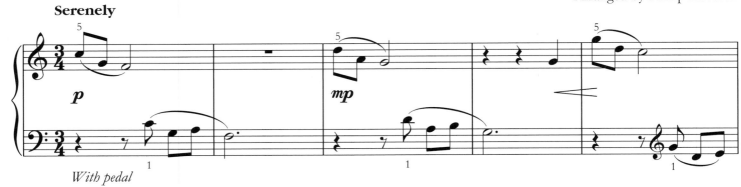

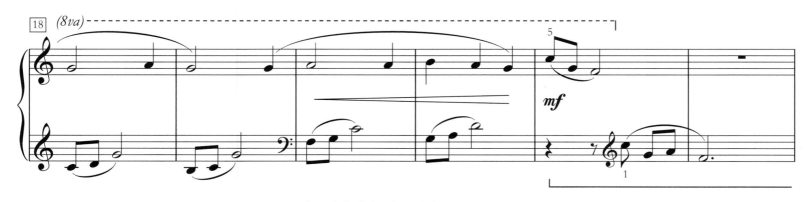

LO, HOW A ROSE E'ER BLOOMING

15th Century German Carol
Music from *Alte Catholische Geistliche Kirchengesang*
Arranged by Phillip Keveren

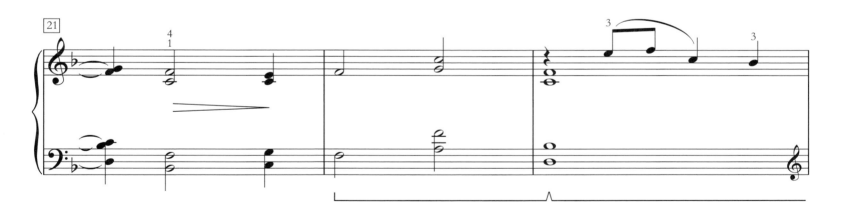

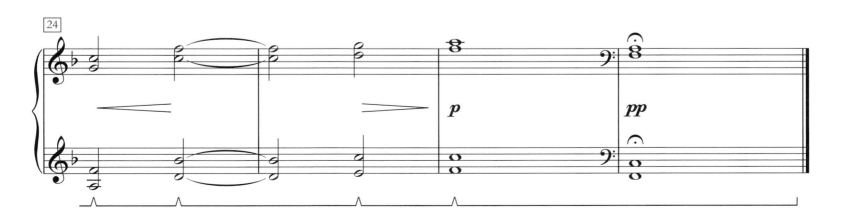

O CHRISTMAS TREE

Traditional German Carol
Arranged by Phillip Keveren

ONCE IN ROYAL DAVID'S CITY

Words by C.F. ALEXANDER
Music by HENRY J. GAUNTLETT
Arranged by Phillip Keveren

SILENT NIGHT

Words by JOSEPH MOHR
Music by FRANZ X. GRUBER
Arranged by Phillip Keveren

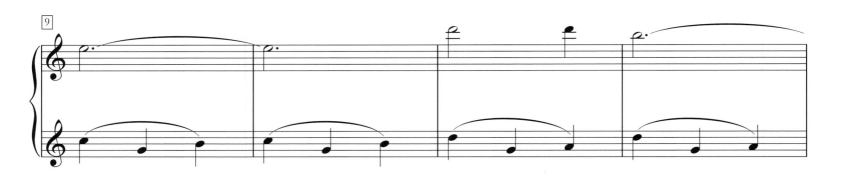

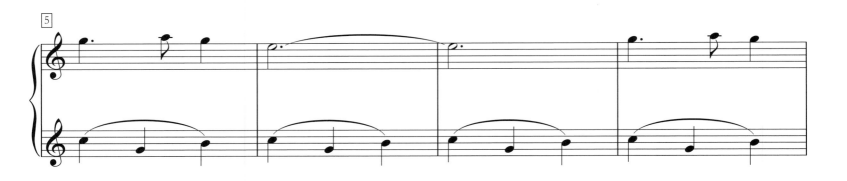

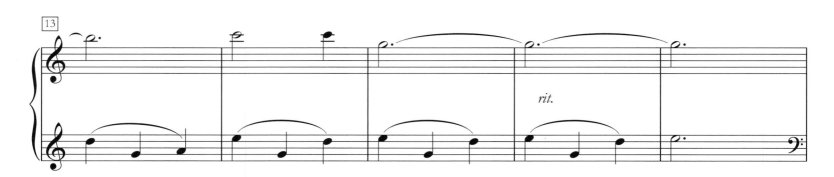

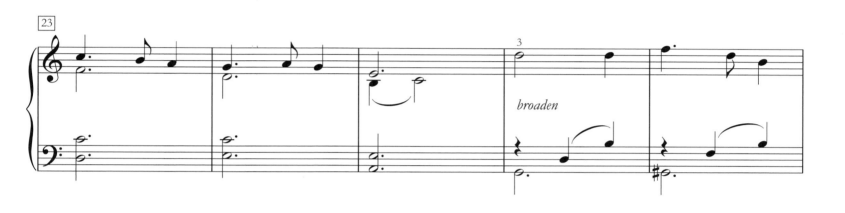

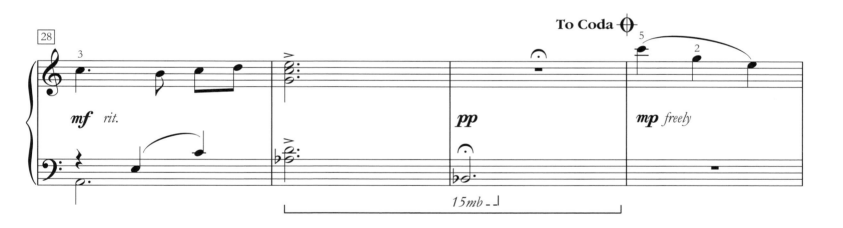

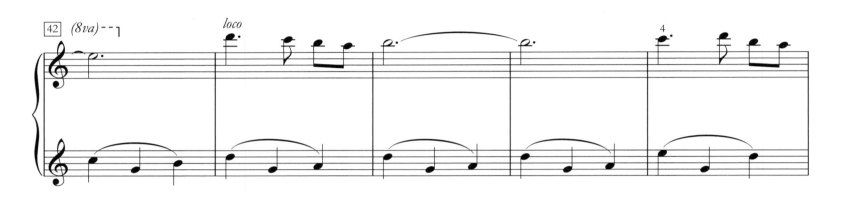

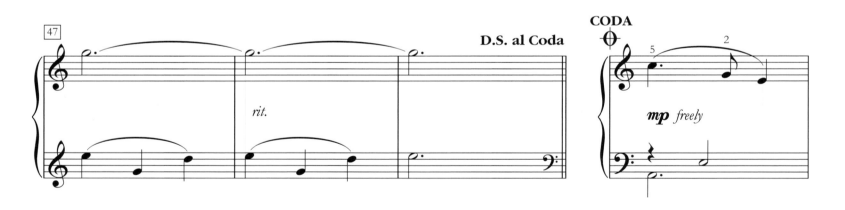

WE THREE KINGS OF ORIENT ARE

Words and Music by
JOHN H. HOPKINS, JR.
Arranged by Phillip Keveren

Steadily, with mystery

mp

With pedal

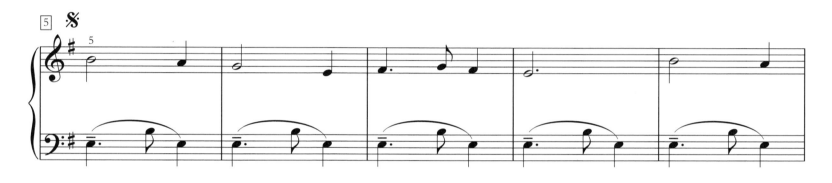

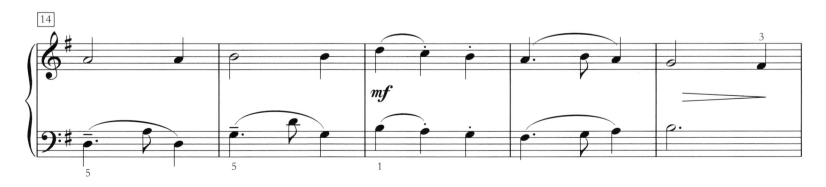

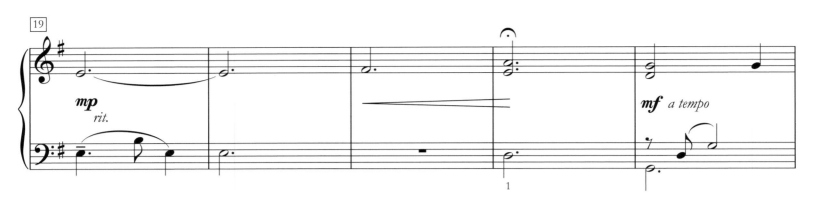

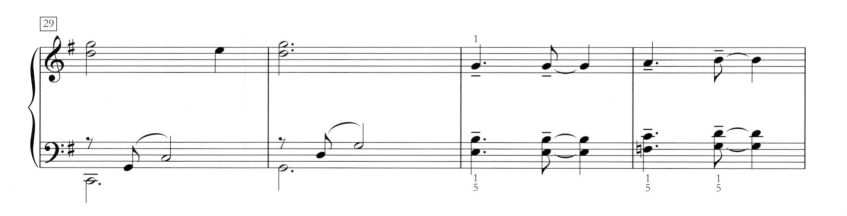

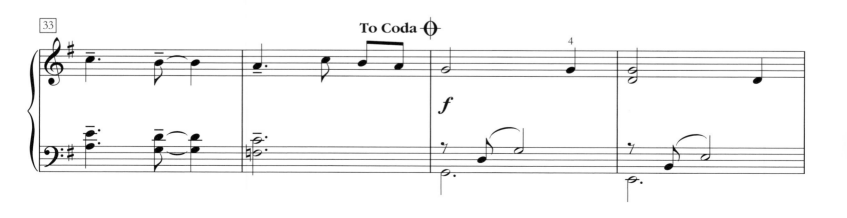

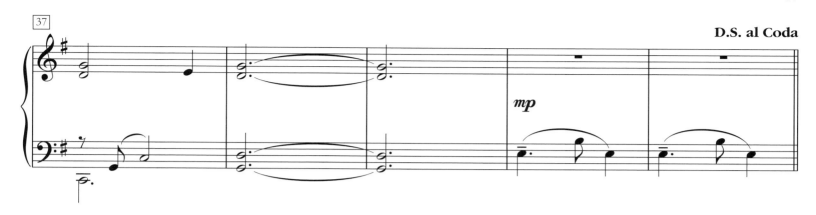

D.S. al Coda

CODA

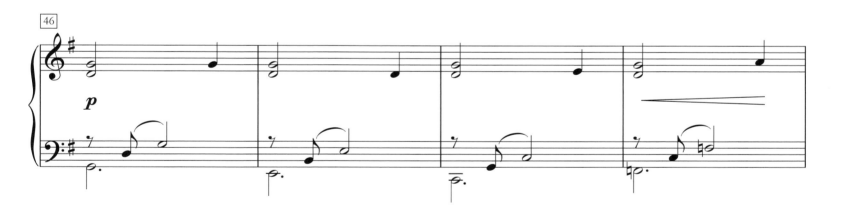

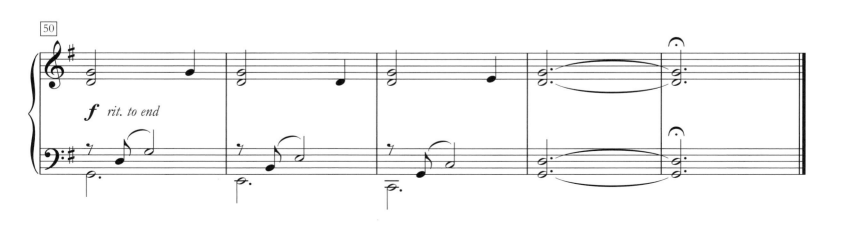

WHAT CHILD IS THIS?

Words by WILLIAM C. DIX
16th Century English Melody
Arranged by Phillip Keveren

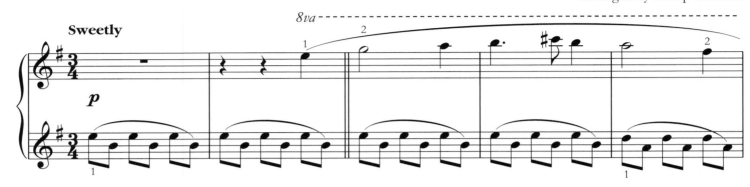

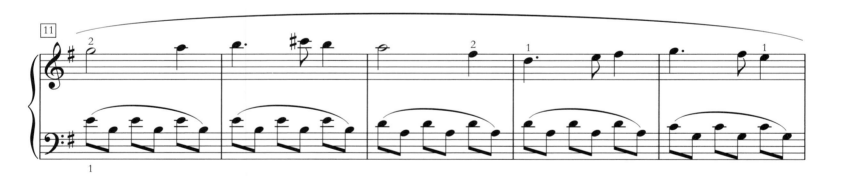

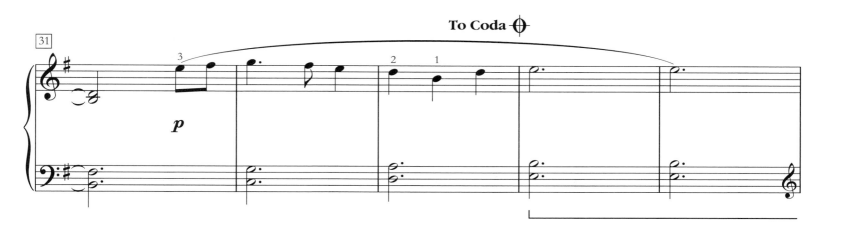

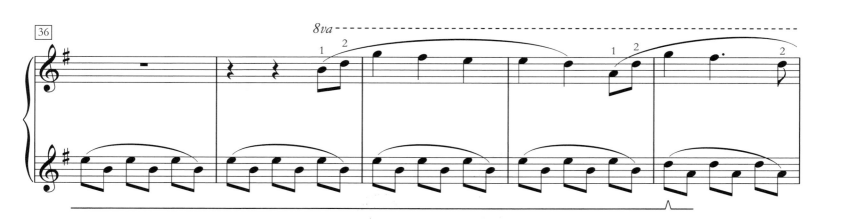

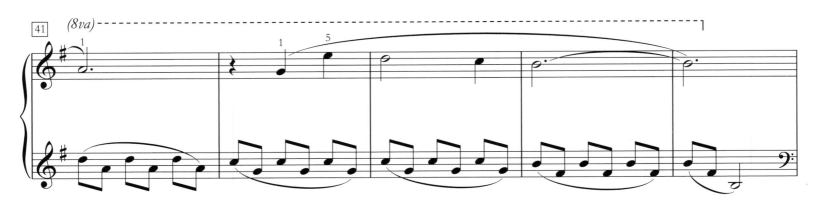

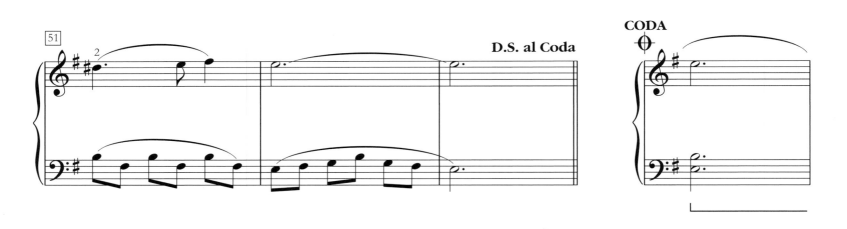

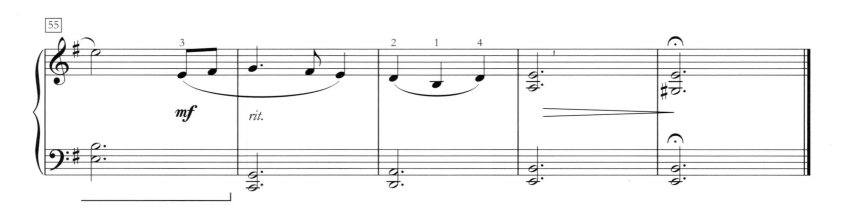